Vikings

Level 10 – White

Helpful Hints for Reading at Home

The graphemes (written letters) and phonemes (units of sound) used throughout this series are aligned with Letters and Sounds. This offers a consistent approach to learning whether reading at home or in the classroom.

HERE ARE SOME COMMON WORDS THAT YOUR CHILD MIGHT FIND TRICKY:

water	where	would	know	thought	through	couldn't
laughed	eyes	once	we're	school	can't	our

TOP TIPS FOR HELPING YOUR CHILD TO READ:

- Encourage your child to read aloud as well as silently to themselves.
- Allow your child time to absorb the text and make comments.
- Ask simple questions about the text to assess understanding.
- Encourage your child to clarify the meaning of new vocabulary.

This book focuses on developing independence, fluency and comprehension. It is a White level 10 book band.

©2023 **BookLife Publishing Ltd.**
King's Lynn, Norfolk PE30 4LS, UK

ISBN 978-1-80505-109-1

All rights reserved. Printed in China.
A catalogue record for this book is available from the British Library.

Vikings
Written by Robin Twiddy
Adapted by Rebecca Phillips-Bartlett
Designed by Danielle Rippengill

FSC
MIX
Paper from responsible sources
FSC® C113515

Image Credits Images are courtesy of Shutterstock.com. With thanks to Getty Images, Thinkstock Photo and iStockphoto.
Cover – Bahau, Ivan Kurmyshov, PRESSLAB. p4–5 – Artindo, El Greco 1973. p6–7 – Drakuliren, drumdredd777. p8–9 – Anna Krivitskaya, Olga Tashlikovich. p10–11 – Always Wanderlust, Anna Kepa. p12–13 – Anna Krivitskaya, El Greco 1973. p14–15 – Olga Makukha, PRESSLAB. p16–17 – Khosro, wjarek. p18–19 – Viktor Osipenko. p20–21 – MMACASSIR, NataliAlba.

Contents

Page 4   Who Were the Vikings?

Page 6   The Gods

Page 8   Family

Page 10   Homes

Page 12   Food

Page 14   Viking Fashion

Page 16   Health and Medicine

Page 18   Being a Kid

Page 20   School and Learning

Page 22   Index

Page 23   Questions

Who Were the Vikings?

The Vikings were a group of people who lived from around 800 AD to 1050 AD. That was almost 1,000 years ago! Vikings lived in part of Europe that we now call Scandinavia. Vikings were not called Vikings when they were alive. They were known as Norsemen.

Vikings lived here

There are lots of stories about Vikings. Some people think that Vikings wore helmets with horns on them. That is not true! Vikings were known for being great sailors and soldiers. They travelled Europe attacking other groups. When they were at home, Vikings were also excellent farmers and fishers.

The Gods

The Vikings had a lot of gods. Just like the ancient Greeks, Romans and Egyptians, the Vikings had gods for all sorts of things. Thor was the god of thunder and strength. Warriors would worship Thor to become stronger before battles. Loki was the god of mischief.

Stories about gods were passed down through poems called the Eddas. There were stories about how the universe was created, how it would end and the battles that the gods fought to keep it safe. There is even a story about Odin giving away one of his eyes.

Statue of Odin

Family

Vikings had very close families. Many generations of Vikings often lived together. Vikings might have lived with their brothers, sisters, parents and grandparents. There could have been between 10 and 20 people living in one home. Vikings also kept many pets, such as dogs, cats, falcons and even bears!

Vikings did not have last names. Instead, they would take their father's name and add the Norse word for son or daughter to the end. So, if you were a boy and your dad's name was Erik, then your name might end up being Erikson.

Homes

Viking homes were called longhouses. Longhouses were just one long room. Most Viking families broke the room up into three smaller areas. One of the areas was used for the family's farm animals. Another area was used as a workshop. This left one space for the family to use.

Longhouses would have a fire in the centre. This fire was used for cooking, light and heat. The ash from the fire was also used to try and stop the longhouse getting too smelly. Despite this, life in a longhouse would still have been pretty smelly and very loud.

Food

Vikings ate a lot of stew. The land they lived on was not very good for farming, so they needed to be good at making their food last a long time. Turning everything into stew was one way that they preserved food to keep it fresher for longer.

Vikings ate lots of meat and fish. They did eat some vegetables, but the vegetables were often put in the stew with meat. Vikings would keep adding to the same stew pot as they took from it, so you could end up eating meat that had been in there for weeks.

Viking Fashion

Vikings put a lot of effort into looking good for each other. Compared to other groups of people who lived at the same time, Vikings were very clean. They bathed once a week, which was quite a lot in those days.

Vikings even wore jewellery!

Vikings were even known to carry little grooming pouches. Inside, they carried tweezers, razors and combs. Most Viking men wore trousers and tunics, which were like long shirts. Viking women wore dresses. However, the very rich Vikings wore clothes made with silk, gold and animal furs from far off lands.

Health and Medicine

In Viking times, it was very important to be strong. They had some interesting ways of trying to keep themselves strong and healthy. Firstly, if Vikings thought that a baby was not going to be strong enough, it is thought that sometimes they would leave them outside on their own!

Once Vikings made it to adulthood, they still had some very weird ways of treating illnesses. When Vikings got sick, some people would try and cure them using a song or poem. This was thought to be a magical cure that would scare away bad spirits.

Being a Kid

Viking childhood was very short. Viking boys were treated like men from 16 years old, and girls were thought of as women from just 12 years old. Viking children were treated just like adults. They were expected to help their family by working on the farm and making food.

Even though Viking children had many jobs to do, they did get to play sometimes. Viking children even had toys, such as wooden swords, bows and toy ships. As well as being fun, these toys were also used to train children for becoming adults.

School and Learning

Vikings did not go to school. However, even though there was no school, there was still plenty for Viking children to learn. Viking children had to learn how to read and write. Instead of using letters, Vikings wrote in shapes and symbol called runes.

Runes

Since there was no school, there were also no teachers. This means that Viking children were taught everything by their parents. Viking children would learn how to do the same things their parents did, such as cooking, sewing and farming. They were also taught poems, songs and stories about history.

Index

farmers 5
horns 5
Odin 7
pets 8

poems 7, 17, 21
runes 20
Scandinavia 4

How to Use an Index

An index helps us to find information in a book. Each word has a set of page numbers. These page numbers are where you can find information about that word.

Example: balloons 5, 8–10, 19

Page numbers

Important word

This means page 8, page 10, and all the pages in between. Here, it means pages 8, 9 and 10.

Questions

1. What were the Vikings known as when they were alive?

2. Who is the Viking god of thunder?

3. What toys did Viking children have?

4. Use the contents page to find out about Viking fashion.

5. Use the index page to find out what animals Vikings kept as pets.